Random Thoughts

Snapshots of the Soul

Rishi Chavan

BookLeaf Publishing

India | USA | UK

Made with ❤ on the BookLeaf Publishing Platform
www.bookleafpub.in
www.bookleafpub.com

Dedication

To the three women of my life,
My grand-mother, my mother & the love of my life.
You are my inspiration, my support, my critic, my
driving force.

Preface

A thousand thoughts per minute,
Some wise, some absurd, some disturbed within.
The human mind, a jumble of emotions,
A kaleidoscope of fragmented notions.

These thoughts, a reflection of my mind,
A snapshot of moments left behind.
Whispers in the dark, confessions to the air,
Loud declarations, shouts beyond compare.

Honest, unfiltered, and unapologetic,
The thoughts that keep me up, the ones that haunt me.
Not grand epiphanies or profound revelations,
Just random thoughts, a reflection of my own creations.

A shared human experience, a messy, beautiful ride,
A journey we all embark upon, side by side.
In the randomness of our thoughts, we find,
A sense of connection, a sense of understanding, a sense
of peace of mind.

Acknowledgements

To the pioneers of poetry, whose words have echoed through the ages, leaving an indelible mark on the human experience, I offer my deepest gratitude. Your legacy has inspired generations, and I am humbled to be a part of this timeless tradition.

To my grandmother, whose dreams for me knew no bounds, I wish you were here to see this moment. Your unwavering faith and encouragement sparked a fire within me, and though you may not be with us today, your love and legacy live on through me.

To my mother, whose honesty has always been a beacon of guidance, I thank you for being my rock, my confidante, and my most trusted critic. Your opinions, always laced with love and a desire to see me grow, have shaped me into the person I am today.

To the love of my life, who ignited a spark within me, helping me to find my voice and my purpose, I am forever grateful. Your presence in my life has been a catalyst for growth, and I am thankful for the journey we share.

And last but not least, to the book leaf publishing for giving an oppertunity to a small fish like me to taste the waters of the literature. Without their intiative this book would have remained a draft hidden in a diary stored in cuburd forever.

1. A Passenger's Dilemma

When you looked back through the mirror,
A figure stood still until we reached the corner.
With a sharp turn, the figure vanished from view,
But why did it feel like it was someone you knew?
The pearls of tears rained down through your eyes,
The pain of departure seemed greater than the skies.
It's not easy to leave everything behind,
While keeping the unfolding future in mind.
Maybe you could have turned back,
Maybe the courage to tell the truth I lacked.
While you stepped on the throttle,
I sat quietly, thinking like a genie in a bottle:
"Is this the road you should take?
Is this the decision I should make?"
Though we were no longer strangers,
In that moment, and even now,
I was, and always will be, nothing but
A fellow passenger, which I cannot forget.

2. Toxic Temptation

How long can I carry this poison in my heart?
Your love is toxic, like a devil's cherry.
Your hypnotic smile, your soothing voice,
Your piercing eyes filled with deception.
You are a siren in disguise,
Spilling nothing but lies.
Your love is toxic, like venomous snake bites.
Like a fool, I adored you,
Like a servant, I worshiped you.
Like a crook, you robbed me,
Like a lamb, you slaughtered me.
Like the ruins of a city, reduced to dust in the ground,
Your love is toxic, like an erupting volcanic cloud.
You were my world, my reason to live,
You were my soul, my desire to breathe.
You were my strength, my purpose, my goodness,
But when you plucked my heart out,
The truth finally dawned that your love is toxic,
And it's destroying us.

3. Hollow

You used to complete me,
Comforting me with your gentle soul.
Your scent lingers in my room,
The rose you planted still blooms.
In gloomy days, I recall
The warmth of your loving palms.
Your voice echoes, clear and bright,
As if you're calling me tonight.
Every space in our home feels bare,
Every room, a hollow space without you there.
I sense your existence, faint but true,
But without you, my heart feels empty too.
The empty space once filled by your belongings,
An empty heart craving your loving.
Wherever I look, I see your vanishing shadow,
Whenever I realize that you are gone,
I become nothing but hollow.

4. Essence & Presence

We sat together, silently,
As the rain poured down outside, wildly.
Our hands entwined, a gentle grasp,
Her head on my shoulder, a peaceful clasp.

I listened to her every breath,
Lost in the warmth of our silent depth.
No words were spoken, no questions asked,
Yet in that moment, everything was tasked.

Perhaps sometimes, it's not what we say,
But our presence that speaks louder each day.
Being there for someone, fully and true,
Is the essence of love, shining through.

5. The Storm Within

She looked at the sky full of stars
While sky looked at her soul full of scars.

She saw how stars twinkled like fireflies
While sky saw her eyes filled with agony & cries.

With constant lies, her heart had grown cold
Moonlight lit up the emptiness she'd been told.

She felt the cold breeze reaching her from the sky
In her the sky sensed the pain, fighting to break free,
from inside.

The tears started to flow from her eyes
The rain started to pour from the sky.

She yelled in agony, Sky roared in fury
She wept, screamed & cursed, Sky cracked, crumbled &
burst.

Soon the floods of emotions receded within her mind
Soon the clouds dispersed & sun started to shine.

Skys heavenly eyes desended down, only to find her free

from sorrows,
She looked up to the sky, with renewed hope of better
tomorrow.

6. The End of Us

Away you go, Oh dearest of mine,
Without a word, without a sign.
Go far away, so never to be mine.
Take with you your smile, your joy, your sorrows, your
cry,
Your existence, your scent.
Take away all the love we shared,
So that never again we both have to pretend.
Don't turn around to look behind,
To witness a broken relation slowly crumbling and
fading away.
To hear my world decay and die away.
Just walk away from me,
Onto your future, beautiful and divine.
Promise me that you will not return,
To seek what once was yours,
To find whatever ruins are left of mine.
Move on in your path, rise and shine.
Leave this empty darkness forever and ever, only to be
mine.
Away you go, Oh dearest of mine,
Without a word, without a sign.
Go far away, so never to be mine.

7. Togather, but not forever

As we stood together, I inhaled your maddening scent
with lungs full,
And memorized each detail of you as much as I could.
The curiosity, anxiety, pain, and countless emotions
Kept ravaging my heart like the waves of the ocean.
I kept glancing at you, only you, hopelessly,
While you kept staring at the love of your dreams for
countless moments.
With each passing second, you drew closer to it,
And with each exhaled breath, I was driven farther from
you.
I tried to bind you with my imaginary bonds,
But you kept leaping forward like a moth to a candle.
I pleaded, yelled, cursed, and burst into a thousand tears,
But how would you know the turmoil hidden inside my
heart's thousand layers?
In between those tormented times, suddenly you held
my hand,
And brought me back into this mortal land.
With sparkling eyes filled with millions of stars,
You asked, "Is he the one for me?"
Knowing our time together had ended at last,
I nodded in approval, just to see you smile,
And as you leaped towards your love, I faded away into

exile.

We were meant to be together, but not forever.

8. If I Could Say It

I saw you even when I looked away—
in the quiet boy who never asked for more,
who stayed even when I left
without a word worth staying for.

I said money didn't matter.
But truth is, I feared
you'd see through what I couldn't offer—
a heart still learning to be brave.

You gave without question.
You helped without pride.
You loved me slowly,
and I—
I came back unsure,
not knowing if I missed you
or missed how you made me feel real.

We spoke of homes,
of nameplates and futures
like we were scribbling dreams
in the margins of a life
neither of us fully owned.

When I said, "Don't leave me,"
I meant: I'm afraid you'll stop waiting.
When I asked for a place beside you,
I was hoping you'd still have space for me.

I liked you—more than I let on.
But I feared you'd ask
why I waited so long to say it.

So here's what I couldn't voice—
not then, maybe not ever:

If you still want to walk beside me,
please know...
I might not know the road,
but I want to learn the way,
with you.

9. Hold On

My soul is not one sound—
it is silence that listens,
thunder that breaks,
and whispers that linger
long after the room has gone still.

I would kiss you in a storm,
not to defy the rain,
but to prove that even chaos
can be tender when held right.

There is a star out there—
unnamed but unforgettable,
a bruise glowing in the sky,
echoing the first time I broke
and didn't know how to heal.

My love?
It smells like lavender.
Like calm after fire.
Like letters never sent
but always meant.

And to the me

who fell the hardest
and never quite landed,
I would say—

Hold on.
Not forever.
Just long enough
to rise again.

10. The Wounds of Words

Someday. Somewhere. Sometime.
You may come to see—
The blame, the curse, the accusations
You cast upon me
Across the years
Were never mine to bear.

Yet—
Every day. Everywhere. Every time.
I believed—
The guilt, the shame, the degradation
Heaped upon me
Were always mine to hold

11. The Way You Are

I love the way you are,
Your smile, your scars.
When you meet my eyes with that steady gaze,
I'm lost in your charm, adrift in a haze.
In your arms, I find my sweetest place;
In your presence, I breathe in peace and grace.
I love the way you are,
Your smile, your scars.

No one's perfect—not the sun or moon—
But hearts that break don't stay apart too soon.
Then someone comes to heal the cracks,
And gently guides your spirit back.
That's what you are—a love so tight,
You hold me close through dark and light.
You're mine—not just in flesh and soul,
But in every laugh, each tear you hold—
A piece of my whole.

Each sorrow and joy, each risk and care,
Each fall and rise—a love so rare.
They are mine too, for you are mine,
In every heartbeat, every line.

I love the way you are,
Your smile, your scars.

12. The Quest

Get into a cocoon,
Hide away from the sun.
When someone seeks you,
Away you must run.

How long can one live,
Trapped in their own making?
How long can one hold their breath,
Each second from escaping?

Don't you tire of your mundane life,
Of being the constant copy-paste?
Don't you feel your curiosity dying,
Living each moment without a taste?

To what extent can this façade last?
To what end can this colossal, hollow structure of the
body endure?
So, if you are content with the status quo,
Then you must not seek what you want to know.

But if you covet freedom,
From the shackles of the mind's servitude,
Then:

Get into a cocoon,
Like a caterpillar, to emerge as a butterfly.
Hide away from the sun, like a shadow,
To become a night that swallows.
When someone seeks you for fun,
Away you must run,
To be born again and again and again.

13. Silent Longing

What is it that you hold within your heart,
What is the secret you keep hidden, apart?
Why today, are you so silent and still?
Why are you quiet, against your own will?

When asked, you only smile,
In laughter, you hide pain all the while.
You become shade under the blazing sun,
Giving all without asking, to everyone.
Why today, are you so silent and still?
Why are you quiet, against your own will?

Is this bond a burden you now feel?
Does my face now seem strange, unreal?
Has this connection lost its charm?
Is there someone more dear, someone who harms?
Why today, are you so silent and still?
Why are you quiet, against your own will?

14. Can Snoring Be Peaceful?

You must be insane to withstand
The rumbling of the throat,
The flapping of the nostrils,
The absurd continuity of the bizarre.
Yet it can be peaceful if
Earned after sleepless nights,
Gained from countless labor,
Forged within the weary lungs.
Then yes, even snoring can sound peaceful.

15. Tossing

Tossing and turning
Throughout the night,
Constantly thinking,
What ifs and what mights.
No way to be found,
No ending in sight,
Endless fears circling
The carcass of the mind.
It won't be enough,
Whatever you do;
The only way forward
Is to go through.
It's always so lonely
When you reach the top.
How much farther will you go
Without knowing when to stop?
Crushing and cursing, life goes on.
Whatever fate holds,
We have to live on.

16. True Essense

We both sat silently,
Rain poured outside violently.
Holding hands together,
She rested her head on my shoulder.
I listened to her every breath,
Diving into the captive embrace.
Neither did she say anything,
Nor did I ask anything,
But we understood everything.
Maybe sometimes, being present
Is love's true essence.

17. Blazing Glory

We danced hand in hand.
We danced until we couldn't.
We were crazy for each other.
We were free together.
We screamed, shouted, and cursed.
We dreamed, laughed, and cried.
We floated like clouds.
We tore down the walls of doubt.
We hugged like it was our last breath.
We clung to each other until we reached the depth—
The depth of our love,
The death of our feelings.
We, the untold story,
Ended in blazing glory.

18. Distance

t was 2 in the night,
The bus dropped me where silence bled,
No one else, just the howling light,
Of distant dogs and paths ahead.

Steps faltered, my heart did sway,
The stillness slept like stone and clay.
The street lamps glared, cold eyes below,
The serpent's path, a lifeless flow.

The wind, a child with fleeting grace,
Played upon rooftops, kissed my face.
A shiver ran, but I let go,
Unzipped my jacket, warmth to know.

Long had it been since I had felt,
An embrace, the comfort I had dealt.
Yet memories tugged, like ghostly strings,
Of that summer night when parting stings.

A flash of headlights, swift and bright,
Vanished back into the night.
"No use in dwelling on the past,"
I whispered, but the thought held fast.

The wind, it shifted, cold and bold,
Towards the city, bright and cold,
Where skyscrapers rose, defying time,
And I wished you were there, yours and mine.

The corner came, the house we'd dreamed,
A memory where once we'd gleamed.
I saw you sit, in your old chair,
Waiting for me to return there.

But fate had called, and I was late,
And you had gone, sealed by fate.
Had I arrived, perhaps to say,
Goodbye, to hold you one more day.

I paused, the gate before my eyes,
Waiting still, beneath the skies.
Life's strange to teach us loss too late,
When all we have is time to wait.

I wished the night would never end,
For wishes, too, just twist and bend.
I looked again, but you weren't there,
Just the empty chair, the empty air.

And as the dawn began to rise,

I found you lost beneath the skies.
You in your life, me in mine,
A ghost of love, lost in time.

19. Words On Strike

People ask me why I can't write.
To them, I say my words are on strike.
My words refuse to imagine:
On a rainy day, a sunny noon;
On a clouded night, a sky with a full moon;
On a frozen winter morning, a lavender bloom;
On a summer beach, a thundering monsoon.

People ask me why I can't write.
To them, I say my words are on strike.

My words cannot see
The need for whispering knowledge through pages,
The wisdom they could bestow like wise sages,
The courage they give to endure for those locked in
cages,
The comfort they bring to hearts that rage.

People ask me why I can't write.
To them, I say my words are on strike.

My words cannot utter
The unspoken truths of society,
The unshackled determination of humanity,

The unquestioning clarity in a world of insanity,
The unhinged defiance of profanity.

People ask me why I can't write.
To them, I say my words are on strike.

My words aren't mute;
They are the screams of an animal deeply wounded,
The echoes of endless possibilities confounded,
The mighty yet grounded mountains,
The lust for eternity of my soul, which is hounded.

Yet, people ask me why I can't write.
To them, I say my words are on strike.

20. The Ship of Theseus

You take something
And replace it with another.
You remove one thing
And hope to make it better.
You rewrite everything
And dream of creating something greater.
Who gave you the power to steal?
Who gave you the right to kill?
As you replace, little by little,
A piece of myself,
As you remake, day by day,
The image of myself,
You rob me of my existence,
Like the Ship of Theseus.

21. Reverie

You are the ocean,
I am just a raindrop, vanishing into you.
You are the sky,
I am just a cloud, floating within you.
You are the storm,
I am just the wind, revolving around you.
You are the volcano,
I am the fire, burning inside you.
You are the mountain,
I am the waterfall, plunging into oblivion from you.
You are the end,
I am an extinction, beginning from you.